SNAKES
in the
PULPIT

CAROLYN WILCOX

CREATION
H O U S E
A STRANG COMPANY

SNAKES IN THE PULPIT by Carolyn Wilcox
Published by Creation House
A Strang Company
600 Rinehart Road
Lake Mary, Florida 32746
www.strangbookgroup.com

This book or parts thereof may not be reproduced in any form, stored in a retrieval system, or transmitted in any form by any means—electronic, mechanical, photocopy, recording, or otherwise—without prior written permission of the publisher, except as provided by United States of America copyright law.

Unless otherwise noted, all Scripture quotations are from the New American Standard Bible—Updated Edition, Copyright © 1960, 1962, 1963, 1968, 1971, 1972, 1973, 1975, 1977, 1995 by The Lockman Foundation. Used by permission. (www.Lockman.org)

Scripture quotations marked CEV are from the Contemporary English Version, copyright © 1995 by the American Bible Society. Used by permission.

Scripture quotations marked KJV are from the King James Version of the Bible.

Design Director: Bill Johnson

Cover design by Justin Evans

Copyright © 2010 by Carolyn Wilcox
All rights reserved

Library of Congress Control Number: 2010933290
International Standard Book Number: 978-1-61638-220-9

First Edition

10 11 12 13 14 — 9 8 7 6 5 4 3 2 1
Printed in the United States of America

Dedicated to my godly grandmother, Hazel Westfall, whose life bore witness to service, survival, and Christ's love.

To all who have been used, abused, and deceived by snakes and wolves in the pulpit and to those who are locked in a personal prison of bondage, guilt, and shame: my prayer for you is to find rest, forgiveness, and freedom in Christ.

May I tell you why it seems to me a good thing for us to remember wrong that has been done to us? That we may forgive it.[1]

—CHARLES DICKENS

Contents

Acknowledgments

I WANT TO HONOR RON, my husband of over forty-six years. You have been my greatest, and often only, support and encouragement in my many days of struggle. Your love, patience, listening ear, and steadfast faith kept nudging me to stay the course and keep the faith when all I felt was despair. You have given me four wonderful children, and now we have seven beautiful grandchildren. I love you.

I am very grateful to my Aunt Carol, a writer with a depth of knowledge, wisdom, and understanding who was kind enough to share with me. You shared with me your struggles and experiences in an honest, open way. Thank you for your inspiration.

To Christi, my daughter-in-law, thank you for taking time from your busy schedule to work on the manuscript for this book.

To my father, grandfather, and all the preachers in my life—good and bad—you have caused me to fall on my knees searching for truth, value, and forgiveness. After a lifetime of guilt, shame, and resentment, I can now say I feel blessed to have had a grand heritage of being a preacher's daughter.

The words of Joseph in Genesis 50:20 (NASB) say it best:

> As for you, you meant evil against me, but God meant it for good in order to bring about this present result, to preserve many people alive.

To God be the glory!

Prologue

THERE ARE OVER 3,000 species of snakes. They have hidden fangs, keen vision, and are paramount at camouflage; snakes are masters of disguise. When we are first introduced to the snake or serpent (later identified as the devil) in Genesis, we get a glimpse of his character and goals. The Bible does not give us a detailed physical description of the serpent while he visited our first parents in the Garden of Eden. We can, however, understand that he had the ability to stand upright and communicate with humans. Interestingly enough, he approached the unique, perfect, and beautiful human that Adam called woman. The snake used God's platform and God's words to begin a dialogue with this woman—Eve. He overrode God's authority and established his own. "No, you'll not die," he prods in Genesis 3:4 (author paraphrase). Then, in complete harmony with the nature of a snake, he went for the strike: "Your eyes shall be opened" (3:5, KJV). He, the serpent, cleverly takes our attention away from God and cunningly redirects it toward ourselves—just enough to cause us to falter.

There are so many unanswered questions about that first encounter with the serpent, but God chose to leave them unanswered. Even so, the serpent is repeatedly revealed to be crafty, cunning, and destructive throughout the Bible. Clearly, the snake is a symbol of the mystical. The snake is an established enemy of God.

In Genesis we also learn that "the serpent was more crafty [subtle, cunning] than any beast of the field which the LORD God had made" (3:1). In the last book of the Bible, Revelation, the serpent's identity is revealed more fully: "And the great dragon was cast out, that old serpent, called the Devil, and Satan, which deceiveth the whole world; he was cast out into the earth, and his angels were cast out with him" (12:9, KJV). Although he is not always called by name throughout the text, his work—temptation—is present from the beginning to the end.

In Matthew 6:23 (KJV), Jesus reminds us: "But if thine eye be evil, thy whole body shall be full of darkness." The eyes of a snake can see the weak and the vulnerable, yet it is also within its nature to pursue stronger prey.

Jesus rebuked the scribes and Pharisees, the religious leaders of His day: "You serpents, you brood of vipers, how shall you escape the sentence of hell?" (23:33). The Contemporary English Version words it this way: "You are nothing but snakes and the children of snakes!" (CEV). What strong words Christ uses to describe those in position to give spiritual guidance! He calls them hypocrites. Peter tells us, "For the time is come that judgment must begin at the house of God" (1 Pet. 4:17, KJV). Lately, a common warning from the pulpit for believers is: Beware the secular world! Perhaps our wariness should also extend toward the very proclaimers of the good news.

Deception, manipulation, robbery, and sexual immorality can (and do) plague the sacred office of the clergy. Many believers struggle to separate God's voice from man's (the clergy, or men of God, who claim to be the voice of God). These spiritual guides are supposed to be God's representatives. But there are snakes in the pulpit. How can we know? Whom do we trust? How far do we follow? Where do we turn?

If you have been bitten by a snake or fooled by an impostor—a wolf dressed as a sheep—in the pulpit, this book is for you. If you have been hurt by the church, this book is for you. I pray that sharing my experience will encourage you to seek the One who is the answer for our healing. There is a cure, or perhaps I should call it an antidote, for your hurting and poisoned heart. It can be painful (at first, the healing process often is), yet powerful and freeing.

> I searched for a man among them who would build up the wall and stand in the gap before Me for the land, so that I would not destroy it, but I found no one.
>
> —Ezekiel 22:30

Getting to Know You

A Generation of Vipers

I T STARTS AT BIRTH. The moment a human is born, it is helpless; a baby has an unspoken need to be loved, valued, and heard. Similarly, a baby bird newly hatched in the nest requires the protection of his mother's watchful eye, lest he become prey for a hungry, stronger bird perched nearby. *Every* creature can be prey, a victim of plunder—even humans. The Bible tells us that man has dominion over the beasts of the field, but who can protect us from the beasts in the pulpit?

THE PREY

I was an unassuming little girl raised in a Christian home with a pastor for a father. My father's business was viral: it invaded every aspect of our lives. Our home was run—as many were at that time—with the understanding that children were to be seen and not heard. I would even say that, for our family, that old adage did not fully encompass the hierarchy in our house. Perhaps an appropriate amendment would be: "And not even really *seen* unless seen doing something profitable for the church." That was life as I knew it, and I lived it faithfully, unaware that a snake, the impostor in the form of a crafty, sensual man—a pastor—with a keen eye for a weak and vulnerable child, slithered into my life.

MY FATHER

My relationship with my father was...well, I really didn't have one. He was the authority figure and a man of few words (at home). My father rarely spoke directly to me, preferring to communicate through his sermons and my mother, so I ultimately understood what he expected. More than once I was corrected publicly from the pulpit.

As a teenager I realized my gift of music, and I became the choir director at our church. Under my direction our choir was invited to sing at the largest church in our district. We accepted the offer and were honored to perform for such a large audience. After the performance the pastor commented on how well we did and even suggested we sing at "headquarters." It was a great compliment. It took two whole days for my mother to tell me, "Your father's buttons were popping out of his chest at the meeting the other day." I assumed that was her way of telling me he was proud. Nothing else was ever said about that.

I remember feeling envious of other girls who freely approached their fathers. I'd watch them sit on their fathers' laps, embraced by their fathers' strong, comforting arms. It's funny how small things can mean so much to children. When I was sixteen my sister was born, and my father was completely different around her. It was as if she was his daughter and I was an adopted stranger living in the house. To this day she refers to herself as "Daddy's little girl." Sharing stories of our father is almost impossible—I don't know the man in her stories, and she is unfamiliar with the man in mine.

I remember hearing my father try to put our relationship into words. I was married with four children, and our family attended my father's small church. On one particular Sunday morning, Mother's Day, 1981, my father was giving gifts to the mothers in the congregation. I received a gift for having the youngest child. He began his presentation by saying, "Carolyn and I have an unspoken, I guess you could say, *respect* between us; but she has been faithful to the church." With that attempt to recognize me publicly, he exposed our relationship or lack thereof. I still have the plaque he handed me, and I can still see my father standing at the podium trying to find the words to say.

As I've grown older I've realized there may be more behind why he was the way he was. My father was one of twelve children, and his father was also a preacher. I saw my grandfather as a selfish, grumpy, miserable, and stubborn man who ran the aisles of his church preaching a hellfire and brimstone sermon with the best of them. I know it couldn't have been easy to be raised by him, but I saw that my father respected him for his stubborn faith. I loved and respected my father, too. He had a relentless and determined faith; he relied on the Word of God and took his calling seriously. Christ used his sermons to brand on my heart the danger of compromising God's Word. Today, more than ever, I appreciate that gift.

After our children left home, my career as a full-time mother was over. I felt empty. "Now, Lord, what do I do?" I remember praying as I sat in my quiet living room. A voice asked me, "What do you enjoy?" I responded, "I love studying your Word." His answer was simply: "Then preach and teach My Word." "I can't. Don't You know I'm a woman?" He replied, "I know." End of conversation.

It took me three years of questioning and verifying to answer His call. At the end of that period, I told my husband what I was to do. He replied, "You know you will have to face your father. Are you ready for his reaction?" By this time my faith was strong. "I know. I can handle it."

The opportunity came when I was visiting my parents' home. I found my father talking with a Christian, male friend about churches and preaching. This was my moment! I shared, and in my own feeble way, I told them *I* was called to preach. My father's response was a devastating, heart-stabbing, cruel statement about women in the pulpit. I was stunned! I sat there numb for a few seconds—barely able to hold back tears. Then I left and drove the seven-mile stretch between our homes, blinded by tears, and eventually—miraculously—arriving home accident free. I parked and ran into the woods that lined our property. Weeping bitterly, I asked the Lord, *begged* Him, to take away my desperate need for my father's love and acceptance. I asked Him to cut the cord. And He did. He answered my prayer. At that moment the Lord gave me the strength and desire to please Him and Him alone.

In the years following, my husband and I were involved in another ministry, and our relationship with my parents was strained. My father voluntarily retired early, after over thirty years of preaching, due to strong dissension in the church. After his retirement the church went through several pastors who all but destroyed any spiritual foundation he had laid.

I eventually heard that his church was without leadership, so I, trembling with fear—but with the assurance of God's call— presented myself as a candidate. Unknown to me, God with His merciful hand was about to perform a miracle. Through unbeliev- able circumstances *I* was voted into the pastor's position of the church my father built. On my first Sunday my father was in atten- dance. Several weeks went by without a word from him, until one day he approached and said, "I could not have done a better job myself." It was his unique way of showing appreciation and respect for me. Previously, I would have fallen apart at his recognition; but God had cut the cord, and I was able to simply say, "Thank you." I saw this as God's gift of grace and an answer to my prayers.

My father died not long after that, but I did enjoy his (brief) encouraging presence and support. I think God wanted to teach me not to rely on flesh, but to completely place my trust and confidence in the One that had kept me all these years from destruction. As the title of my old favorite hymn says, "He Is All I Need."

MY MOTHER

My mother was a perfectionist and a fierce protector of her husband. She was, and still is, a strong, hardworking perfectionist in the truest sense of the word. She set high standards for herself, my father, and the rest of us. She is multitalented, and I grew up watching her pursue her interests and responsibilities with precision. She cleaned, cooked, sewed, canned, hosted, taught, and entertained for her family and her congregation all while raising three children. She always sat staunchly in the front row of the church in obvious agreement with my father and his ministry. To many twentieth century congregations, she would have been considered the consummate minister's wife. I was a child with my own struggles, questions, fears, and imperfections; I never quite felt that I fit into her world. She had all the Martha skills, but never shared them with me. She didn't have the patience to teach me, and besides, there was too much risk for failure. All I knew to do was stay out of her way as best I could in order to bring no shame to the image she and my father had created.

My mother was a protector, too. She lived and breathed the ministry, and she did everything in her power to protect it. She was skeptical, mistrusting, and guarded; and I realize now that a lot of that may have evolved as a result of my father's authoritative control and high expectations. She never allowed for honest, open dialogue, as it would have possibly exposed signs of frailty or sinfulness. Nothing was going to destroy her husband's ministry—not on her watch. In her eyes it would be unpardonable for someone to disagree with my father or his decisions. Of course, of this *I* was guilty. Even today my mother remains faithful, holding the banner high for herself and their ministry in order to please God. I love her and honor her dedication and lifetime of service to my father and his work.

THE PASTOR'S DAUGHTER

I was about two years old when my father entered the ministry. As the years passed I grew to understand that the congregation held an important place in the life of my family; and eventually I understood that those who paid tithes were the really important ones. My father did not show affection for me, neither publicly nor privately. My preacher father never told me those words every child craves to hear: "I love you." My parents did not believe in complimenting children lest they get a "big head." Love—or I guess acceptance— was conditional in accordance to its benefit to the church folk. It's interesting how children learn to survive in challenging environments. In general my goal was to avoid rejection and keep peace with the people of the church. My personality was to joke, have fun, and make people happy, while maintaining a religious righteousness. I knew it would be pleasing to God to please and follow my father, His divine spokesman. Regularly I heard (and still hear today) the often-taken-out-of-context, yet popular, Psalm 105:15 (KJV), which reads, "Touch not mine anointed." I realize now that this is an example of a scripture being used to foster fear, giving control and the ability to manipulate others to those who quote it out of context. If I displeased the preacher, my father, or brought any disgrace to his name or ministry, it was a sin against God. And God would punish. This was so ingrained in me during childhood that it took well into my adult years to flush the idea from my body and mind.

As a child with an intense desire to be loved and valued, I was an obvious and easy target for a crafty and cunning snake. I remember my first encounter with a snake. It was a night service at church camp. I sat captivated in my seat, surrounded by other preteenagers, swept up by the atmosphere and captivated by the words of a talented, charismatic, lovable preacher. I drank in every word; he spoke with such love to us kids. When his eyes met mine, I thought "Wow! He really cares for me!" I still remember the simple prayer he taught to us children that night. He said, "When words fail you, simply pray, 'Lord, help me!'" I didn't know it then, but he was a deceiver, a wolf in sheep's clothing, a snake; and he was utilizing his keen senses to set the stage for a strike.

Unlike the kids of today, many kids of my generation were naive—even ignorant—of the facts of life. To use the word *sex* was to curse. I actually do not recall ever hearing the word spoken aloud until I was much older. So great was the fear surrounding that word (fear instilled by my father? Fear instilled by God?), that I felt it created a wall of protection around me. I know now that it was the hand of God.

I need to stop here for a moment and say that no matter what profession you may be in or environment in which you were raised, evil snakes and wolves can be and have always been present in positions of authority. When those in power are associated with God or godliness, it adds a completely different dimension. Jesus called out a "generation of vipers" (Matt. 23:33, KJV) over 2,000 years ago. They were the religious leaders of the day, and they presented themselves as the righteous. A *viper* is defined as "a venomous, old-world snake; a spiteful, treacherous person."[1] Who would not do everything in his or her power to run and seek protection from a viper?

What can be learned from Jesus' words, particularly those used to describe certain religious leaders? In yet another passage Jesus warns His disciples using the metaphor of a wolf. Matthew 7:15 says, "Beware of false prophets [teachers, preachers], who come to you in sheep's clothing, but inwardly are ravenous wolves." *Ravenous* is defined as "covetous, devouring, predatory, greedy, and wolfish."[2] Wolves are known for running in packs dominated by an alpha pair. The pack cooperates to snare larger prey such as deer, but they most often target a young, old, or weak member of the heard, pursuing it until it is exhausted.

When snakes and wolves share pulpit time, the thrill of the hunt yields its fleshly reward, and power and control tastes sweet on their tongues, like candy. The world tells us that wealth and power equal happiness; and it can be difficult to resist the lure of big, flashy companies and attractive get-rich-quick seminars. Although we Christians are called to be different, sometimes the church promotes the clergy and the pulpit as a means of wealth, power, and happiness at the expense of the unsuspecting prey, the sheep—the animal Jesus used to describe His followers.

Snakes kill their prey by suffocation without breaking a bone and can change skin color as a defense mechanism. Wolves run their prey into exhaustion; and we all know the saying, "a wolf in sheep's clothing." For both of these animals, the goal of the disguise (deceit) and pursuit is to fulfill a desire—hunger. In the animal kingdom this is perfectly acceptable, the way God intended it. Among men it is evil. Is there a graveyard for the people who thought life was found in the church or clergy? Where do we bury our dead? Where do the victims of snakes and wolves go for help? What twenty-first century preacher wants an exhausted, penniless, suffocated person as a member of his or her church? A person dying the death of disappointment and disbelief is not exactly a top recruit for most churches today.

The deceived are left to struggle. I know the daily fight a victim or survivor goes through. For me, it was a war within myself: I felt I was dying slowly while fighting for freedom and truth. I asked, "Is anyone real anymore? Is God real?" I felt suffocated, and for me that meant a life lived with guilt, shame, unworthiness, and rejection. I thought that if God is only man's voice and man is God's only voice, then, I have no hope. Where are the healers? Where is truth? Can anyone be trusted? I rested in Psalm 23:1:

The LORD is my shepherd, I shall not want.

2

Living in the Garden

Having Eyes to See

Y HUSBAND, RON, AND I have been doing missionary work in Kenya since 2002. Shortly after we began our work, we had the privilege of meeting an English lady who was in Kenya doing social work. We met under rather unusual circumstances, during a rough period in her life. She informed us that she was an atheist; she understood we were Christians, nonetheless a friendship formed and grew. We shared many of the same experiences, being foreigners in a very different culture. Our common ground was our desire to know and reach out to the wonderful people of Kenya.

On a beautiful, hot Kenyan day, our new friend approached us saying she heard of an animal preserve just a few miles out of town. Her adventurous spirit and contagious enthusiasm made it hard to resist when she asked, "Would you like to go check it out?" Ron and I responded, "Great! Let's go." We got a late start after trying to catch a *matatu*, or passenger van, that not only had space for the three of us but also was going in our direction—not always an easy task. If you've never experienced a *matatu* ride before the new

10

codes were in place, let me tell you that it is an adventure in itself. In what is meant to be a nine-passenger van, we have counted up to thirty beings—adults, children, chickens, etc.—packed together inside. That number does not include the "hawkers" hanging out the doors, no matter how hot or humid the day. Eventually we found one that would take us toward the animal preserve.

We were dropped off near a dirt road where a small sign assured us we would find some wild, African animals. Waiting here was our next mode of transportation—a bicycle taxi, or *boda-boda*. Several young Kenyans with single-speed, old-fashioned style bikes lined up, hoping to make a few shillings for their day's wages from these three green *mzungus* (white folks). I think the bikers had a competitive spirit, for our next wild ride began as the strong legs of our Kenyan bicyclist raced the others. It seemed mile after mile passed—did we get the directions right? There were no signs, but then again, it was Kenya. The thrill of the ride, the wind, and beauty of the countryside did however override the fresh odor of perspiration wafting back toward us.

We finally reached our destination and sought information at the small guardhouse, anxiously awaiting our tour of African animals in the wild. We were assigned a guide who told us that because we arrived well into the hottest part of the day, we may not see very many animals, as they tend to retreat back into the forest to avoid the heat. "It is better to come early in the morning," he told us. We really didn't want to hear that after the unbelievable difficulty we experienced trying to get to the preserve.

Our guide graciously took us on the tour through the forest and shared about the animals that lived there. We didn't see even one. Our initial disappointment began to wane as we walked, carefree and unsuspecting, along the trail surrounded by a dense, quiet blanket of trees and brush. Suddenly, as quick as the blink of an eye, a large, black snake appeared at our feet; it looked like our American boa constrictor (the ones that squeeze their prey to death). We're not sure who was more surprised—we or the snake—for our shrieks, screams, and scurried steps sent the snake back into the bush as quickly as he appeared. Our guide named the species, but in our excitement I failed to commit it to memory. Be assured, I walked and followed our guide more carefully back to the building.

Snakes (serpents) with their slithering, camouflaged bodies often appear suddenly when we aren't expecting them. In the Garden of Eden surrounded by beauty, provision, and the presence of God, the serpent appeared to Eve. No wonder Jesus uses the word *beware* so often as He instructs His unsuspecting sheep.

My "preserve" during my young, formative years was also on a dusty, dirt road lined with only five houses, a general store, and a small, white church with a steeple. I could walk to my one-room schoolhouse shared by eight grade levels. In the middle of the school was a big, black, potbellied stove. About a quarter mile from the school was the outhouse (wood toilet holes). I had one teacher who had one paddle, and she managed to keep us all in our seats until our grade level was called to the front for participation. This was my Garden of Eden. It was what people now consider the good ol' days, and we did feel safe and secure. It was there, in *my* garden, that the snakes would begin their squeeze, preparing the way for complete deception.

My brother and I felt a responsibility to stay out of the way, to allow the ministry to carry on. Our parents had very little interest in the daily drama of our adolescence. We were country kids and innovative for sure; we used whatever was available outdoors as our "toys." Roads, trees, barns, snow—all were settings for creative adventures. It was a great way to grow up. Today, of course, technology has changed that for most kids. The old saying, "An idle mind is the devil's workshop," still rings true, though.

As I said earlier, being pleasing to others was a tool in my survival kit. I was a typical child with a need to be loved, valued, and regarded. We don't grow out of this; these needs only deepen with age. It is amazing how a snake sees the vulnerability of its prey. I learned how to fight and struggle with all the strength a little girl could muster, mostly out of fear, from the molesting of the big boys at church.

Preachers and evangelists frequently came for revival meetings and stayed at our house. I guess the purpose of revival was to stir up the dead saints into living holy. Some (not all, of course) were snakes in the pulpit in need of revival and holy living themselves, who instead played tag with a vivacious little girl. Their flirtatious looks, touches, and comments passed over my head as I naively, ignorantly, and desperately sought to please these men with my fun-loving personality. By being pleasing, I won favor and acceptance from those visiting preachers, thereby pleasing God and hopefully my father.

I wondered why my mother was so tough on me; she instilled in me a great fear of God's judgment. Was it only to keep me from bringing any shame to the ministry? Did she also live under such pressure? As life went on, the answers were revealed. Only those who have experienced it can understand the control, fear, and domination that someone can impress upon a life when misusing God to gain an inappropriate advantage. Snakes use God for ungodly purposes. With this fear instilled in me, I knew—or thought I knew in my young mind—when the line had been crossed. Fear strengthened me at a young age; however, I see it was really God and His provision that prepared me for my future encounters with snakes and wolves.

I was only two when my father was given his first church after returning from the war. It was a shoebox of a church in the cold, snowy North. We soon moved to the quiet, country living of the small community I described earlier. I've heard my mother retell the story countless times: my father, attending Bible school under an exempt status, was sent off to war after questioning a certain doctrine put forth by his Pentecostal teachers. He went to the head of the college saying that he felt he could not preach what was being taught, and maybe he wouldn't be a good representative of that denomination. The response they gave him was: "If you will not preach for us, you'll not preach for anyone." He was turned in and sent off to war.

Despite my own struggles and disagreements with my mother, I've tried to put myself in her shoes. She was a young mother with a son and newborn baby girl living alone in a rented basement. Her husband was in Germany, a soldier sent to war by the church—not the government. Would he ever return alive? I wonder if we were orphaned now, would the church have cared for us? In my experience, I'm afraid I know the unfortunate answer to that question. In the Bible, James says that to care for the fatherless and widows in their afflictions is pure religion before God (1:27, KJV). God, the preacher man, a church organization: Were they one and the same? Would anyone dare put on the church doors, "Warning! Snakes and wolves reside here! Beware! The bite is deadly!"? Yet Jesus did just that when He sent out His disciples. Matthew 10:16 (KJV) says, "Behold, I send you forth as sheep in the midst [pack] of wolves: be ye therefore wise as serpents and harmless as doves." Here Jesus tells us the serpent is wise (cunning, crafty) and the dove simple, harmless—even naive. In 2 Corinthians 11:3, Paul warned the church at Corinth, "But I am afraid that, as the serpent deceived Eve by his craftiness, your minds will be led astray from the simplicity and purity of devotion to Christ." Today, we use words like *hypocritical* and *evil* to describe those in the secular or sinful world; but Jesus used similar epithets such as *vipers* and *serpents* to describe the *religious leaders* of His day.

There are myriad types of snakes all over the world. Especially in India, snakes are known for their beauty and ability to be handled; it's not uncommon to see one twisted about the body of even a young child. Many serpents have the ability to be manipulated—to be everything to everybody. Again, I quote Jesus' words as He goes further in His warning and calls the vipers "false prophets," which tells us they were preachers and teachers spreading a religious message. In Matthew 7:15 (KJV) Jesus tells the multitude in His Sermon on the Mount, "Beware of false prophets, which come to you in sheep's clothing, but inwardly they are ravening wolves." Here Jesus gives us another clue by saying "which come to you." Can you or I remember when we have heard a message on the masquerade of prophets coming to the people? Sadly enough, too often it is the woman who finds herself a snake's prey, just as in the Garden of Eden.

In the Garden—that beautiful place of safety, the place children can play without fear—the serpent appears. Similarly, in the church—that place of the holy presence of God, where souls have come to find forgiveness, rest, peace and safety—the serpent appears.

> He makes me to lie down in green pastures; He leads me beside quiet waters.
>
> —PSALM 23:2

15

3

The Bait

Did God Really Say That?

ONE OF MY FAVORITE books by Phillip W. Keller is *A Shepherd Looks at Psalm 23*. In his book he establishes credibility as a subject-matter expert with his experiences. He writes that he grew up and lived in East Africa surrounded by simple native herders whose customs closely resembled those of their counterparts in the Middle East. As a young man he made his own livelihood for about eight years as a sheep owner and rancher. His experience has given him firsthand knowledge of sheep, their nature, and their management.

As I said before, the sheep is the animal that Jesus uses to describe His followers. In John 10:14 (KJV), Jesus uses a metaphor to identify Himself and His followers. He says, "I am the good shepherd, and know my sheep, and am known of mine."

From Phillip Keller's book I want to list a few of the characteristics he gives of sheep:

- No creature strays more easily than a sheep.
- No animal is so incapable of finding its way back to the flock when gone astray.

- Few creatures are as defenseless as sheep.
- Without a shepherd, sheep are exposed to be devoured by wolves, dogs and other wild beasts.

Sheep do not take care of themselves as some might suppose. More than any other class of livestock, they require endless attention and meticulous care from the shepherd. He goes on to say that "ravens often attempt to destroy a small lamb by picking out their eyes. When thirsty, sheep become restless. An ill-fed sheep is ever on its feet trying to satisfy its hunger."[1]

No wonder the Bible says, "Be of sober spirit, be on the alert, Your adversary [enemy], the devil, prowls about like a roaring lion, seeking someone to devour" (1 Pet. 5:8). At the beginning of that same chapter, Peter gives instructions to shepherds to "feed the flock of God" (v. 2, KJV).

While in Kenya my husband and I saw real-life examples of the behavior of hungry sheep (literally and figuratively). We were amazed to see very young children shepherd sheep through the streets; and witnessing it brought Biblical times alive for us, giving the parables of Jesus deeper meaning. In the more impoverished areas of Kenya, both the shepherd and the sheep are often very undernourished and constantly on the move to find greener grass.

One day on our walk to town, we witnessed the birth of a lamb on the side of the road. It was feebly trying to stand and walk on its own. After awhile we saw a young lad pick up the frail lamb and carry it in his arms, so as not to slow the flock down. It was another living example of how Jesus searches out the lost and afflicted, carrying us because we are unable to walk on our own.

Jesus, however, has returned to His Father; and the scripture tells us He has placed great responsibility on those He calls as His under shepherds. He told Peter, "Feed my lambs" (John 21:15,

KJV). *Feed* My sheep; not starve, not abuse, not rob, nor run them ragged, but *feed them*.

In the tenth chapter of John, Jesus tells us of a hireling (one who works for money not for love of vocation); he sees the wolf coming and flees (v. 12). Today people are flocking to churches eager to hear the messages of wealth and prosperity coming from the pulpit. The seekers then wallow undernourished, hoping for a new revelation or book to give their lives meaning. The sheep become the prey for the wolves and cunning snakes.

I was one of those little lambs under the care and nurture of a shepherd. I was one of those told repeatedly that *the* Shepherd and *a* shepherd were one and the same. And that shift of God's words by the master linguist, Satan, makes some sheep believe: "That is what God really said...wasn't it?"

> He restores my soul; He guides me in paths of righteousness for His name's sake.
>
> —PSALM 23:3

4

The Bite

The Serpent Is Craftier Than Any Beast

No one sues righteously, and no one pleads honestly.
They trust in confusion and speak lies; They conceive
mischief and bring forth iniquity. They hatch
adders' [snake of the viper family] eggs and weave
the spider's web; He who eats of their eggs dies, And
from that which is crushed a snake breaks forth.

—ISAIAH 59:4–5

I WAS ELEVEN YEARS OLD when my father took his first church in the city. Though our environment changed, the world my parents created for our family remained the same. Our church world was as far removed from the outside, sinful world as our country living was from city living. Preachers, church services, choir practices, Sunday school, and revival meetings all kept us separated from the sinful world. In comparison to present day, there was indeed a definite separation of the church from the world back then. The separation was made distinct mainly by rules and the constructs of denomination. The esteem of that adherence and structure often resulted in pride and self-righteousness.

I do believe in separation, but by Christ's teachings and not man's organizational decrees. Jesus spoke again to religious leaders and called them hypocrites when He said, "This people draweth nigh unto me with their mouth, and honoureth me with their lips; but their heart is far from me. But in vain they do worship me, teaching for doctrines the commandments of men" (Matt. 15:8–9, KJV).

While my parents were busy creating and maintaining the church world that dominated our lives, I was growing up—experiencing young life, going to school, and trying to survive those treacherous years of adolescence. My parents seemed unaware or ambivalent of my growing pains, for ministry was their priority. I believe in the truth of Scripture, that God is to be first place in our lives, but I couldn't reconcile this inconsistency. Unless one lives in a monastery, the life we live for God is lived out in love with those around us. Ministers and missionaries (along with their children) have long struggled with this balance.

The charismatic, loving evangelist that I mentioned in the previous chapter had captivated many hearts along with mine. Gaining in popularity, he was now our state's representative of evangelism for our denomination. He traveled from church to church to encourage growth and renewal. Regularly he and his wife would stay at our house when they traveled; and as a result of those meetings, a strong friendship grew between our families. I loved them, they loved me, and I couldn't do enough for them. Serving them was like serving God.

Now, as a young teen, I viewed this pastor/evangelist/friend as the loving, attentive preacher father figure I so desperately needed. I was comfortable with his overly loving gestures, and—as any naïve, little girl would be, I was totally unaware of the implications. Let me say that if any married man—especially a preacher—had touched or acted in this manner toward our daughters, we would have pursued charges of inappropriate sexual conduct with a minor. At the time, to me, this did not seem out of the norm.

The evangelist and his wife had been married for a few years and had prayed that God would someday bless them with a child. We were all thrilled when we heard the news that God had answered their prayer, and they were expecting their first child. When it was revival time at our church, my father invited this effective, talented minister and his wife for a week's worth of meetings. By this time his wife was in her last month of pregnancy. I served them in any way I could; that was my nature. I had a desire to please.

In ministerial terms the meeting was successful. Allow me to describe that last night in my impressionable, pubescent mind: Preaching behind the pulpit was this mighty man of God, attractive, talented, charismatic, and on fire for the Lord. His message and style were gripping as he stood, holding up his Bible, telling us to become revived and live holy. As he was preaching he would also speak in tongues.

The baptism of the Holy Ghost (evidenced by the speaking in tongues) is the doctrine that sets the Pentecostal denomination apart from others. My purpose here is not to deny or defend that doctrine, but to emphasize the warning Jesus gave to His sheep about snakes and wolves as false prophets. A snake in the pulpit may use the gift of tongues to create the perception of validity and godliness. In this case, the abuse of the gift gained the wolf control over the sheep.

The congregation was revived! The altars were filled with men, women, and young people—myself included. Everyone was crying and intensely praying. I was seeking God to give me what this preacher had—what I *needed* to live holy before God. We wanted to be like him! He was God's man, God's voice, and God loved him. This is the problem seekers still face today: we are not quite sure—is it him or *Him* we really want to be like?

I wish I had been aware of the scripture found in 2 Corinthians that says, "No wonder, for even Satan disguises himself as an angel of light. Therefore it is not surprising if his servants also disguise themselves as servants of righteousness, whose end will be according to their deeds" (11:14–15). I was more cognizant of "touch not mine anointed" (Psa. 105:15), which was interpreted as: question not, disagree not, or God will punish. Yet, no matter how hard I tried to please my father, the other clergy, or the saints, it was never quite right or quite enough. I'm sure every minister's child has faced a similar struggle. In those days the common perception was that holy preachers raised holy children.

The revival ended, and when the evangelist asked my parents if I could go home with them to help his wife in her last days of pregnancy, I was thrilled! I loved to be a servant, and it was an honor to serve the preacher and his wife. I worked hard, cleaning anything and everything I could in order to be as helpful as possible. I should have been wary about his flirtation, or at least suspected alternative motives, but I did not. I was a young, innocent virgin when the charismatic preacher finally approached me in a manner that made his intentions clear. His methods were gross, dirty, and sexually criminal toward an underage teen.

Their small house was furnished by the denomination. A four-inch stud and thin wallboard separated our bedrooms. One night after a long day of work, I went to bed totally exhausted. There was not a lock on my door. As I was drifting off to sleep, my preacher "hero" walked in. I was stunned. He came straight over to my bed and began to kiss, maul, and molest me, as I viciously started to fight and wrestle.

"What are you doing? What do you want? Get away from me!" I tried to yell. He held my mouth to keep me still, as his wife lay just a few feet away next door, asleep in their bed. He became frustrated and very angry with me, and he eventually left the room. In a daze, trying to absorb what had just happened—or what could have happened, I could not sleep. Minutes later, to my terror, he returned. He threw a book at me, barking, "Here! Read this!" It was *not* the Bible.

This "man of God," the one I must please or follow in order to be accepted by God, just shoved a book at me. What did he want from me, this preacher that had stood in the pulpits of many churches across our state? Now, how could I please him, he who was instrumental in soul winning and that had led many children's camps? Like most naive, ignorant young girls who wanted to know about life, boys, and sex, my curiosity was like a parched horse in a desert looking toward a mirage. So, I started to do what the preacher asked, for he wouldn't ask me to read anything I shouldn't, would he? It looked very interesting to me.

Fearful, confused, and curious, I opened the book to the first chapter and began to read. Almost immediately, a deep sleep came over me, almost as if someone had anesthetized me. My mind and my body went numb, and I had no control. The book fell to the floor, and I remained in that deep sleep until morning. I know now that God had sent an angel to protect me. I was very sensitive and impressionable—that book would have sent me on the path of destruction. What was the book? It was a book filled with sexually descriptive encounters. And to think, just a few days earlier, it was the Bible he was telling me to read.

I awoke the next morning with great fear and anxiety. I went about my duties, but the air was tense with very few words spoken. Interestingly enough, excitement was also in the air as the preacher's wife began laboring, and we all knew her time was near. As morning comes, so night follows. As I mentioned, I had no way to keep him out of my room; there was no lock on my bedroom door. Why would I need one? I was in the home of a representative of God. In my mind, I was sure that another episode would not occur as his wife was laboring and about to have their first child.

As I lay in my bed thinking about his wife—great with child, he returned to my room. He was undressed and ready! Once again, ready to molest, attack, and defile an innocent, little girl. I fought again and tried to scream, but I couldn't.

"Get away! What are you doing?" I cried.

"Did you read the book?" he asked angrily, as he became increasingly frustrated that I would not cooperate.

"No! Go away! What are you doing? Please, please leave me alone!" I begged.

I guess he thought that if I had read the book I would have been easier prey. I fought, enveloped in fear, but believing that God's strength would get me through. Frustrated, he threw a childlike tantrum because he was unable to obtain what his sinful flesh desired. God protected me, yet again, against this preacher's attempt to rape and defile me. That night sleep did not come, but morning did.

All throughout my childhood I was surrounded by preachers that I looked up to as role models. I had admired and loved the man who attacked me—the preacher I listened to so intently as he spoke about God's love for me. Yet, he would never speak a word to me again. I felt confused, rejected, frustrated, and not pleasing to anyone. I had failed!

Thank the Lord, his wife was taken to the hospital that same day and gave birth to their first child. I returned home completely paralyzed by everything that had happened. After over forty-five years of marriage, four children, and seven grandchildren, I still cannot find strong enough words to describe a man who preaches God's Word, stands as God's representative, and attempts to rape a child in the room next door to his wife while she is in labor.

Today is no exception, as immorality in the pulpits has become an epidemic. The great New England preacher, Jonathan Edwards, gave a sermon on July 8th, 1741, entitled "Sinners in the Hands of an Angry God." It could aptly be re-titled "Clergy in the Hands of an Angry God." If the fear of God and the need for repentance is gone from our pulpits, it will be missing from the pews. Jonathan Edwards' sermon brought his congregation to their knees in tears and conviction. Whose sermon will bring the preachers to their knees in total surrender and helplessness before God?

I want to quote a portion from Mr. Edwards" sermon:

> The God that holds you over the pit of hell, much as one holds a spider, or some loathsome insect over the fire, abhors you, and is dreadfully provoked; his wrath towards you burns like fire; he looks upon you as worthy of nothing else, but to be cast into the fire; he is of purer eyes than to bear to have you in his sight; you are ten thousand times so abominable in his eyes as the most hateful venomous serpent is in ours. There is no other reason to be given why you haven't gone to Hell since you have sat here in the house of God, provoking his pure eyes by your sinful wicked manner of attending his solemn worship; O sinner! [O Preacher!] Consider the fearful danger

you are in; 'tis a great furnace of wrath, a wide and
bottomless pit full of the fire of wrath, that you are
held over in the hand of that God, whose wrath
is provoked and incensed as much against you as
against many of the damned in Hell.[1]

These are the words of a man whose vocabulary is limited in the
sight of God. Psalm 66:18 (KJV) reads, "If I regard iniquity in my
heart, the Lord will not hear me." The Psalmist David continues to
say in 39:5–6, "Behold, thou has made my days as an handbreadth
[short]; and mine age is as nothing before thee: verily every man at
his best state is altogether vanity. Selah. Surely every man walketh
in a vain shew [image]."

Only Jesus can really give us the words to describe sinful religious leaders who deceive by wearing sheep's clothing: *snakes and
vipers*!

Is that too strong? Listen to God our Father's words while
instructing His people on such matters in the Old Testament,
under the old law:

But if in the field the man finds the girl who is
engaged, and the man forces her and lies with her,
then only the man that lies with her shall die. But
you shall do nothing to the girl; there is no sin in the
girl worthy of death, for just as a man rises against
his neighbor and murders him, so is this case.

—DEUTERONOMY 23:25–26

Listen to Jesus speak to us from the New Testament:

> And whoever receives one such child in My name receives Me; but whoever causes one of these little ones who believes in Me to stumble, it would be better for him to have a heavy millstone hung around his neck, and to be drowned in the depth of the sea.
>
> —MATTHEW 18:5–6

Jesus also says:

> For from within, out of the heart of men, proceed evil thought, adulteries, fornication, murders, Thefts, covetousness, wickedness, deceit, lasciviousness, and evil eye, blasphemy, pride, foolishness: All these evil things come from within, and defile the man.
>
> —MARK 7:21–23, KJV

Through these scriptures, we are shown the mind and judgment of God.

What happened when I returned home? Nothing! Conversation was not encouraged in our home. I kept everything inside. I was to be seen and not heard, and I feared I would be the discarded one. However, within weeks my father seemed stressed about an announcement he was planning to make from his pulpit. I am sure he chose his words very carefully. The truth eventually came out; the beloved evangelist, my attacker, was no longer preaching. It recently had been made public that his wife was not the only woman having his baby.

My father's announcement cut through my heart like a well-sharpened dagger. Was it my feeble understanding of the terrible implications of the other woman or the devastating blow of pure deception? That pastor never did care for me or anyone else—he used his position for personal gain and abuse. I wept bitterly. I was mourning a death externally, but what affected me more deeply was the internal death that was taking place within me.

I remember my mother asking me about my reaction in an accusing manner, but I answered nothing. I buried the people and the incident deep in the graveyard of my heart and memory, hoping it would never be resurrected. No one knew and, seemingly, no one cared and life went on. Could I, at least, win approval from my father? Still experience any love or acceptance from God?

Whether it is a child, an adolescent, or an adult that is bitten (defiled, deceived, betrayed) by a snake in a pulpit, it is a wound that a medical doctor can not heal.

> Yea, though I walk through the valley of the shadow of death, I will fear no evil: for thou art with me; thy rod and thy staff they comfort me.
>
> —PSALM 23:4, KJV

5

Symptoms of the Venom

You Shall Not Surely Die

M ANY HAVE HEARD THE dreadful prognosis from a doctor
of terminal cancer. I can only imagine the reaction a
patient might have: How can this be? I feel fine! My
daily life has not been disturbed. I don't understand. Yet, inside, a
deadly poison is taking over. How long has it been there? Can it be
removed? Doctors don't have all the answers.

My story is neither special nor unique. Many before me have
experienced unbelievable trauma—physically, spiritually, and
emotionally. It is a common human response to bury pain, push it
down to a place where we won't let ourselves feel it anymore. Why
not? Who deliberately wants to go through the experience of pain
and take the time to come out the other side? Especially when all
that hurt is associated with God, where does one turn? "Certainly
not the church," I thought. I didn't have anyone to confide in.

As I mentioned earlier, my father was a strong authoritarian
and frequently discriminated against women, especially in church
matters. Women were the cause of all church problems, he believed.
Their role was to be subservient to their head. They were to cook,

clean, sew, teach children, and help raise funds for the church. My mother, the extreme perfectionist, avoided teaching me domestic skills in order to minimize the risk of failure. Teaching me was not high on her list of things to do.

My heart was drawn to the Scriptures at a very young age. Every little girl looks up to her father, and mine was a preacher. I feared his correction and longed for his affection. My significance, my place, was conditional in regards to my value to the ministry and congregation. I carried this lack of worth and deep desire to be accepted by my father, any preacher, and God into my adulthood. I involved myself in what I knew best, church work and whatever that offered. Once I was married with children, my life took on value in motherhood—maybe I had found my place of identity. Even then, though, I was still being introduced as "the Reverend's daughter." But the cancer, that deadly venom, was there lying dormant and influencing my attitude and every decision I made.

I was a mixed bag of emotions, all at once needing to prove myself worthy (trying to find approval from my father, God's man) and desperately seeking a good pastor (I doubted the authenticity of each and every one I heard speak). I questioned everyone and everything. There is safety in being cautious, but it also can deter peace. Would my cancerous venom affect my children? Hidden hurt is so often mirrored in life lived.

The movie *Yentl*, starring Barbra Streisand, is a favorite of mine and very refreshing to watch. In her role as a Jewish girl, she was to marry, have children, and accept her submissive role in society. Deep in her heart, though, she desired to study the Scriptures—a practice which was reserved strictly for males. The difference between us was that she had her father's blessing: he secretly taught her the Scriptures. The story line painted a vivid picture of my unfulfilled dream.

I knew that pleasing my father was pleasing God. To me that meant I needed to come under his authority and ministry. My husband and I felt that we could and should join him as he began new work independent of his previous denomination. I wanted to be there for him, but it was I who needed his approval. I wanted to be heard, but my simple understanding of Scripture clashed often with his strong, forceful attitude. Was I questioning God? According to my father, yes, I was wrong—not because of fact, but because of position. Two examples come to mind that demonstrate his leadership attitude.

The first example occurred during the time our family served in his church; someone we knew well had minor surgery. It affected my father very personally. Why? He was afraid that this would bring shame to his ministry because someone close to him did not rely on faith and God's power to heal. I could not comprehend such a response. I believe in healing, but in accordance to faith in God—not because of the manipulation, control, and ego of man.

Another example is when we made the decision to leave my father's church. My father and I had disagreements, which had escalated to the point where I could no longer serve under him. Our family needed to serve God without a church-family conflict. The Sunday morning came when we would attend a new church. We were busy getting the children ready when the phone rang. It was my father to inform us—or more correctly—threaten us. On the phone he recounted a time in his previous church when some people disagreed with him. He told us they developed many troubles. One was diagnosed with cancer, and eventually both men died. His message was loud and clear: we would not escape God's punishment. I was both fearful and furious. I was fed up with preachers; I didn't want anyone to know I was a preacher's daughter. I didn't want anyone to know of my Pentecostal background, either. I was ashamed and shamed. It was a low point for me.

Was there really a God?

The new missionary church became a solid blessing, mostly because we thought it necessary to keep the children in church. I could not fathom the thought of failing my children in regards to God. But fail I did in so many ways. Striving to please out of a fear of rejection always brings more rejection. Desiring love while not knowing love results in failed attempts to give love. I began to live in a world of self-condemnation and continual failure. We loved our new church; the people were wonderful, and it just seemed like a fresh, new start for us. I tried to recover while praying God's blessings for my family. I could only do what I had been trained to do all my life—work. Choir, Sunday school, youth, you name it, I participated. We enjoyed a great relationship with the pastor, but as most pastors do, this one moved on. The new pastor was completely different. I enjoyed working with people. My fun-loving, *joie de vivre* ways returned; but I always took God's Word and work very seriously.

One day I was told that the new pastor made a comment about me and our daughter. He described us both as being personable and vivacious, but then he added *flirtatious*. That word hit me like a ton of bricks, and I completely shut down. A woman in the church approached me and asked what was wrong because I seemed down. I couldn't tell her, but later she heard of the pastor's opinion and told me not to worry. It left me asking, "Who am I supposed to be?"

The bite, the shame, the blame of the past overflowed like a broken dam. I could no longer work there for fear I would be misleading and cause degradation to the work of God. I despised myself and everything I represented. I was confused because my motives seemed right, yet my personality seemed wrong.

That pastor's attitude affected all of us. Our kids were now teenagers with friends that attended a church near our home. Those friends and others from school who were active in youth group helped them get connected, grow, and develop their many talents. I never got involved again, but I took pleasure in seeing my children achieve and grow.

One by one, our children began to leave home to find their place in life. Empty-nest syndrome hit hard. The value and purpose I found in motherhood was slipping away. My friends changed; my busy schedule all too quickly became idle. Everything seemed to be changing. Yes, I still had the responsibility of a wife, but my husband's livelihood had mostly remained the same: he worked and he did his chores. He is a hard worker, and he gets great satisfaction from a job well-done. I am not a Martha and finding any job to make money didn't appeal to me. I was a Mary and loved to discuss the Scriptures. But without a formal education or the platform of a preacher's wife, it was difficult for a Mary to find equality in Christ in the church.

After our oldest son left, I turned his basement room into my study. There I totally immersed myself in God's Word. I wanted nothing to do with religion's control, piety, or manipulation. Rick, our youngest and in high school, would joke in his caring way, "Mom, I can always find you in your holy room." And he was right, for it was in that lonely, secret place I cried out. Searching, asking, and praying for God to make me, take me, help me, and break me. When any heart really begins to seek God, that heart had better be prepared for an answer—God's way. Psalms 51:17 (KJV) is a scripture David found to be true: "The sacrifices of God are a broken spirit: a broken and a contrite heart, O God, thou wilt not despise."

Christ, in His merciful, unconditional love and with the sharpened sword of His Word under the care of the Holy Spirit, started the long, painful process of drawing out the buried venom, now decayed with hurt, rejection, bitterness, and the inability to forgive others and myself. I would pray the words of Psalm 119:133–134 (KJV):

> Order my steps, in thy word: and let not any iniquity have dominion over me. Deliver me from the oppression of man: so will I keep thy precepts.

Could I really be loved unconditionally?

> Thou preparest a table before me in the presence of mine enemies; thou anointest my head with oil; my cup runneth over.
>
> —PSALM 23:5, KJV

6

The Prescribed Recovery

And the Eyes of Them Both Were Opened

M Y AUNT CAROL SUFFERED through a painful divorce when her pastor-husband had an affair with a woman in their church. She offered this truthful analysis:

> The preacher's wife has no place to go when this happens; she becomes the outcast. Her identity is in the shadow of her husband's vocation. The distressful drama of finding her place, her niche, can be a devastating experience. She feels suspicious of the church, guilty as the congregation talks, and paranoid that her faults and failures have been exposed. However, the minister, who is good at his profession, is reassigned to another parish or state with blessings to begin anew.

She knew of other women who stayed with their churches while their husbands moved on to new churches. One woman she knew absolutely could not cope; and she died in a mental institution, while her husband was assigned to another congregation.

Aunt Carol shared the following story with me from a "Dear Abby" article in the *St. Paul Pioneer Press*, April 8, 2008.

> Dear Abby,
>
> I'm writing in response to "In True Love in Washington," about the 16-year-old who became pregnant by her pastor. What she described is not a "love" relationship; it is an abusive one. A pastor who has a sexual relationship with a member of his congregation is misusing his power, and this constitutes clergy sexual misconduct.
>
> You were correct when you stated that "if there is any shaming," it should be directed at the pastor. Unfortunately, that is not typically the case. The shaming of victims that follows disclosure is nearly unbearable. Church officials typically collude in denial or cover up the problem. Rarely is there any care for the victim.
>
> For this reason, a sex-abuse therapist and a spiritual director familiar with this type of abuse are helpful in the healing process. In addition, it is vital for the victim and her family to find the support of someone who has lived through clergy sexual misconduct, because it is unlikely they will find support in their current circle of friends.
>
> —C.W., Muskegon, Mich.[1]

My Aunt Carol also gave me permission to share this very personal story:

> The first man who approached me after my divorce was final was a minister I had known and respected.
>
> He said that he had been attracted to me for a very long time, and if I would wait until his youngest child was through high school, he would divorce his wife and ask me to marry him. His utterly outrageous suggestion came out of the blue and without warning, to say the least. He was married, had a lovely wife and four children. He shocked me even further by saying, "I should tell you that you would not be the first one. During the time I was in seminary, I drove to Chicago on Monday and came back to my parish on Friday. During the week, I slept with a woman who lived in the area."
>
> I was incensed and nauseated by his suggestion and perhaps even more by what he revealed about himself.

How would Christ view such situations?

A tradition I enjoy at Christmastime is watching the old movie *Holiday Inn*, starring Bing Crosby. His character in the film tries to restore dignity to his former commanding officer in the Army. The question is asked, what do you do with a leader when he stops being a leader? It's a heartfelt thought. So, I ask, what do you do with a preacher's wife, when she stops being a preacher's wife? This question is applicable to many stations in life, including motherhood and even deceived, hurt, and wounded prey. What does the church do with the bruised?

In the movie's song the answer is given: "We love him! We love him!" If only that were the history of the church in these last decades: We love her! We love her! We love her!

Those of us who are generally labeled "baby boomers" remember all too well the Jimmy Swaggart fiasco. He was a powerful and popular TV evangelist whose spectacular fall was televised throughout our nation. Hearing and watching the disgraceful debacle was, to me, like vinegar for my wounds. Still, Swaggart kept his church and extended ministries and eventually returned to television. That's good, for God is a God of forgiveness. However, what I remember so vividly about those dreadful days is a small picture of a plain, poor-looking woman's face plastered across this country's papers as the woman that brought him down.

Anyone remember her name? Does anyone care? Why did she have to work as a prostitute? Was it to feed her family? To survive or be loved? And what about her soul? That disgraced woman could not turn to the clergy. In her experience they were the snakes lying in wait for their prey.

Similarly, the woman at the well was looking for love from all the wrong men. Jesus revealed Himself for the first time as the Messiah to this woman—giving her freedom, forgiveness, and living water. It was the robed, religious leaders that Jesus called hypocrites and vipers—not the abused, shamed, sick, and lonely. To the latter He gave purpose, and they became His followers. Why? Jesus brought equality. Satan's servants bring oppression.

A Bruised Reed, by T. A. Lambie, MD, is an old book of my father's that has blessed my soul many times. The title is taken from Isaiah 42:3, "A bruised reed He will not break And a dimly burning wick He will not extinguish; He will faithfully bring forth justice." In his book, Dr. Lambie explains that he was asked to go on a tour of the upper Nile. The purpose of the tour was to explore the commercial possibilities of making paper for the world's use from the vast areas of papyrus found on the White Nile. To make the paper they had to bruise or crush the reeds. Natives living on the banks of Lake Tsana in Ethiopia built large canoe-like boats of papyrus. The reeds that had been bruised carried the constricting rope so that it did not slip off and let the boat sink. He compares it to the Christian experience; often it is those who have had the worst bruising who really hold the vessel together and are the greatest source of strength. The bruising is not for punishment but for strengthening.[2] Yet those words are neither comforting nor encouraging during the times of bruising.

For the many like me that have experienced bruising, what can keep us from completely sinking into destruction? For me it was a tiny seed Christ planted in my heart as a very young child. As a child I listened to my father preach hundreds of sermons, but one Sunday something he said stuck with me. It wasn't so much the message as it was just one scripture verse. When Jesus was teaching the multitude in His Sermon on the Mount, He said:

> But thou, when thou prayest, enter into thy closet, and when thou hast shut thy door, pray to thy Father which is in secret; and thy Father which seeth in secret shall reward thee openly.
>
> —MATTHEW 6:6, KJV

In my child's mind I said, "OK. That's it!"

A family we had shared a lot of time with while living in the country had a teenage son. He had stopped going to church and was doing his own thing. I would hear adults talk of their concerns for him. So I took action. Afraid my mother would find out, I waited until she was busy doing her chores; then I would sneak upstairs into my tiny one- by two-foot closet, like the scripture said, squeeze myself in and close the door. In secret I would pray, "Please, Lord, bring back Melvin and save his soul, Amen." I feared being caught. I don't remember how long I kept going to my closet, but I was faithful like the scripture said.

In our country church we had what was called testimony time almost every Sunday night. One typical Sunday night, to my surprise, in walked Melvin. My heart began to pound, although no one was aware of me—the little daughter of the preacher. Testimony time began, and Melvin stood up to say he had given his heart to Jesus and was a part of the Christian family once again. If someone could have seen what was taking place inside of me, they would have sent me home to bed.

Wow! It worked! It's true!

I had prayed secretly, and God rewarded right before my eyes—*openly*. The seed of faith was planted. I am a very private person, never allowing my inward fears, emotions, or thoughts to show. I was never given that opportunity when I was young. But that seed, no one could take that seed away. I never told that story to anyone until Christ asked me to share it in a small, poverty-stricken village in Uganda, some fifty years later.

Peter warns us in the New Testament, "Be sober, be vigilant; because your adversary the devil, as a roaring lion, walketh about, seeking whom he may devour" (1 Pet. 5:8, KJV). Yet another animal metaphor is used—this time it's the lion with power and dominance. The devil, my enemy, would spend my lifetime trying to snuff out that flickering flame of faith.

It was many years later when, again, in that secret closet or holy room, that hurt which I thought was buried was brought to light. I now needed Jesus, the Truth and Life, to unwrap my wounds that bound me in the way Lazarus was bound as he came out of the tomb. Because of that secret closet, I began to allow myself to be fully revealed—to myself and to God. That was the beginning of learning to walk on my own.

Before modern psychology, the psalmist David gave us the first formula to healing. After the prophet Nathan revealed to him his sin with Bathsheba, he recorded God's desire. He said, "Behold, thou desirest truth in the inward parts: and in the hidden part thou shall make me to know wisdom" (Psa. 51:6, KJV). He continued to ask the Lord to "purge me, wash me, make me, create in me, restore me and cast me not away." (See Psalm 51:7–11, KJV.) These are the cries of a broken heart willing to be known to God.

I mentioned earlier my conversation with the Lord in my living room. I began to pray, "Lord, what am I to do?"

"What do you enjoy?" He asked.

"I love studying Your Word," I answered.

"Teach and preach My Word," He responded.

"Lord, don't You know I am a woman?"

"Yes."

And that's where the conversation ended. From that time on I have experienced many challenges, struggles, and painful battles with both victories and defeats. I would go to my secret prayer room, my refuge, at times still struggling with my own self-worth. But, more miracles and changes were on the way.

My husband's company was offering early retirement, and he was eligible. We both felt we needed to make ourselves available for God to use us whenever and wherever He needed us, and this was the first door which opened. After much prayer, the only thing keeping us from being completely available was our home. It had been our home for over thirty-two years and the children's homestead. We knew they looked forward to bringing their own children, our grandchildren, to play as they once did in the beautiful, wooded, five-acre property.

We put our home up for sale, and after seven days on the market it sold; we were essentially homeless after thirty-two years. No one understood why we did it; they thought we had lost our minds. We didn't know what we were going to do or where we would go. We knew God had a plan, so we were ready to wait on Him. We bought a used 1986, twenty-foot camper trailer and parked ourselves at a campground. We're sure it was tough on our children; perhaps they suffered a lost sense of security when the house sold. Surely, having to tell people that their parents were living in a campground was disheartening, to say the least.

As I look back, we had to be the talk of the town. People probably assumed we had slipped over the edge. But for us, walking every day by faith toward the unknown and unfamiliar yielded some of our greatest and most inspirational times together as a couple. In December 2001, we went to Africa with a group of rather wealthy people we did not know, and we found ourselves asking, "What are we doing here? We do not belong." But God is not a respecter of persons, and that trip was divinely ordered and Spirit directed, as evidenced by the several team members who shared about their own pain and struggle for healing.

At a Spirit-guided appointment we spent a morning sharing with a well-known pastor. Unbeknownst to me, my husband had told him of my struggle with guilt and my love of teaching God's Word. I remember his encouraging words like it was yesterday. He said, "God used the Peters as well as Paul to spread His gospel." That conversation led to a private meeting; and for the first time I counseled with a man that represented the ministry. I shared hesitatingly, fearfully, and in fragments my experience with preachers.

I had never trusted anyone with this information. Sharing details with my husband was a bridge I had yet to cross.

From that inspiring trip we ended up doing missionary work in Kenya. And on one of those quiet days with no vehicle, no TV, and no radio to distract us, I unloaded my burden on my husband. I told him of the night God protected me from rape. Through my tears I told him that if that preacher would have succeeded in raping me, I would have been disowned by my family. Additionally, I would have gone down a path of destruction because no one, I felt, not even God, would have wanted me. He knew me well enough to agree wholeheartedly; God had protected me. I had crossed a hurdle.

We never talked about it again. I had won a personal battle by sharing, and it was time I moved on—until June 22, 2009, which I call my miracle day. It was an ordinary day; the Lord woke me up at His usual time of 5:30 a.m. I did my daily devotion, and then I stepped outside to enjoy the beauty of the sunrise, which always reminds me of God's faithfulness. After a moment of reflection, I went about my daily chores. Ron had left earlier to do a handyman job for someone, but I saw that he had returned. He was still sitting in his car listening to the radio. When he came in I gave him my usual welcome home, and then he said, "I've got something I want to tell you."

He was very serious. My heart skipped a beat. He had been listening to a story on NPR (National Public Radio). It was a story of a woman my age who was a preacher's daughter. She told of the pain, loneliness, and abuse she suffered. Our stories were very similar. Her story opened his heart, and he said, "I want to say I'm sorry for not understanding better, for not being more sensitive, for not being there for you all these years. I want to be here for you and understand better."

I was speechless and overwhelmed. We both started to cry. What I had inadequately attempted all my life, God accomplished in one day. There was love, understanding, and value without condemnation. It was as if a bright light was shining through a window, and I basked in it all day. That God would do that for me was unbelievable!

One woman, after many years of pain, decided to share over National Public Radio, and her story helped unlock mine. It made a difference in our home and in my life that day. If she could do that and help someone she would never meet, maybe this unimportant, uneducated preacher's daughter could help set free a woman who is locked up in the prison of her mind from the deadly poison of a snake in the pulpit. That would be worth it all!

I never did hear "I love you," those words a daughter longs to hear from her father. But in his last days of life, I know I gained his respect for being a woman who loved God and His Word. I loved my father and appreciated his preaching, for in all of his sermons he would emphasize the power and truth in the unchanging Word of God. His lifetime of ministry library was my treasured inheritance.

Epilogue

Watchman Nee in his book *The Release of the Spirit* opens the chapter named "The Importance of Brokenness" with a powerful statement. He writes, "Anyone who serves God will discover sooner or later that the great hindrance to his work is not others but himself."[1] My life is proof of that.

To the many holy men and women who stand in the pulpit week after week underappreciated yet faithfully spreading the good news of Christ's love, I applaud you! I pray daily God will call more like you for the future generations, for we desperately need you.

We can neither change our disappointment in people nor turn back the clock, so the only option for living life after being bitten by a snake in the pulpit is to keep moving forward. Life is a forward kind of word, and to live means another sunrise, another day. Jesus is the healer of hurt, anger, bitterness, and feelings of worthlessness. The only prescription I have found to alleviate my pain is to find a secret operating room, and completely bare yourself in the presence and care of the Master Surgeon.

To every person who has been bruised, my question is: "What kind of a Christ have you formed in your mind?" Is it the real one from the Holy Bible, one painted on an oil canvas by the artistry of man, or Satan's snakes and wolves that pose as ministers of righteousness standing in the pulpits?

> For you were continually straying like sheep, but now
> you have returned to the Shepherd and Guardian of
> your souls.
>
> —1 PETER 2:25

If you have been poisoned by the clergy (snakes in the pulpit) or wounded by a church (religion), be careful; do *not* discard the cure they've offered in Christ. Wrap yourself completely in the arms (person) of Jesus, God's Son. Life, love, and freedom are found there!

> Surely goodness and mercy shall follow me all the
> days of my life; and I will dwell in the house of the
> LORD for ever.
>
> —PSALM 23:6, KJV

About the Author

CAROLYN WILCOX HAS BEEN involved in Christian ministry for over fifty years. She has served as music director, youth leader, teacher, pastor, and for the last eight years as a missionary in Kenya. While living in Kenya, she held Worth of Women conferences, taught relationship classes, and conducted pastor training sessions in various villages.

Lapidoth Ministry supported Carolyn's Kenyan friends in building their first church structure. This church has become the headquarters of three other churches. Lapidoth Ministry shares in their large vision of someday having an orphanage, widow complex, and school, which are very much needed in these extremely impoverished villages.

Lapidoth Ministry also works alongside an organization called God Sees Men and Women in Africa. This outreach is mainly to train and encourage women in their struggles and hardships of everyday life.

Carolyn is the founder of Anna's Club—Bridging the Gap, a concept that she would like to share with your group or church to help pass the baton effectively to the next generation. She welcomes the opportunity to teach, preach, or simply share her testimony with your group or church. Also, if you would like to share your thoughts and experiences you can contact her at:

lapidothministries@gmail.com
www.snakesinthepulpit.blogspot.com

Bibliography

Cooke, Fred, Hugh Dingle, Stephen Hutchinson, George McKay, Richard Schodde, Noel Tait, and Richard Vogt. *Encyclopedia of Animals: A Complete Visual Guide*. Berkeley, CA: University of California Press, 2004.

Dickens, Charles. *12,000 Religious Quotations*. Grand Rapids, MI: Baker Book House, 1989.

Edwards, Jonathan, *Sinners in the Hands of an Angry God and Other Puritan Sermons*. Mineola, NY: Dover Publications, Inc., 2005.

Keller, Phillip. *A Shepherd Looks at Psalm 23*. Grand Rapids, MI: Zondervan Publishing House, 1970.

Lambie, T. A. *A Bruised Reed*. New York: Loizeaux Brothers, 1952.

Nee, Watchman. *The Release of the Spirit*. N.p.: Sure Foundation Publisher, 1965.

Resnick, Jane P. *Snakes: Photo-Fact Collection*. Boston: Kidsbooks LLC, 2008.

The World Book Dictionary. Chicago, IL: Field Enterprises Educational Corp. 1974.

Notes

DEDICATION

1. Charles Dickens, *12,000 Religious Quotations* (Grand Rapids, MI: Baker Book House, 1989), 146.

CHAPTER 1—GETTING TO KNOW YOU

1. *The World Book Dictionary*, 1974 ed., s.v. "Viper."

2. *The World Book Dictionary*, 1974 ed., s.v. "Ravenous."

CHAPTER 3—THE BAIT

1. Phillip Keller, *A Shepherd Looks at Psalm 23* (Grand Rapids, MI: Zondervan Publishing House, 1970), Introduction, 35–36.

CHAPTER 4—THE BITE

1. Jonathan Edwards, *Sinners in the Hands of an Angry God and Other Puritan Sermons* (Mineola, NY: Dover Publications, Inc., 2005), 178.

CHAPTER 6—THE PRESCRIBED RECOVERY

1. Response to "Dear Abby" article found at http://findarticles.com/p/news-articles/news-item-the-shamokin-pa/mi_8154/is_20080408/dear-abby-im-response-love/ai_n53658209/ (accessed July 11, 2010).

2. T. A. Lambie, MD, *A Bruised Reed* (New York: Loizeaux Brothers, 1952), 24–25.

EPILOGUE

1. Watchman Nee, *The Release of the Spirit*, (n.p.: Sure Foundation Publisher, 1965), 9.

LAPIDOTH

MINISTRY

"IT'S NOT ABOUT GENDER,

BUT FAITH AND SURRENDER."

"FOR THERE IS NO RESPECT OF PERSONS WITH GOD."

ROMANS 2:11